STRANGE DAYS AHEAD

also by Michael Brownstein

Behind the Wheel
Highway to the Sky
Three American Tantrums
Brainstorms
30 Pictures
Country Cousins

STRANGE DAYS
AHEAD

by

MICHAEL BROWNSTEIN

Z PRESS

CALAIS · VERMONT

1975

Acknowledgements: Some of the poems in this book first appeared in the following publications: *Adventures in Poetry, The American Poetry Review, Big Sky, Chicago, Collection, Fits, 49 South, The Herald, The Paris Review, Poetry, Rolling Stone, Shanti, Sitting Frog, Stooge, The Ant's Forefoot, Telephone, TriQuarterly, Two Charlies, University Review, Unmuzzled Ox, The Village Voice, The World, Z,* and in *Another World* (Bobbs-Merrill), *Statements* (George Braziller) and *Dial-a-Poem* records.

Front cover photograph by August Sander

Back cover photograph by Gerard Malanga

Photograph on page 85 by Nathaniel Dorsky

COPYRIGHT © 1975 BY MICHAEL BROWNSTEIN

LIBRARY OF CONGRESS CATALOG NUMBER 75-26450

ISBN: 0-915990-01-6

For my parents

Contents

In 1857 when a warship, the Maracanha, *made its first appearance on the Paraguay River a party of Indians paid her a visit; and on the following day they were seen to have drawn anchors all over their bodies. One Indian had gone so far as to cover all the upper half of his body with a complete representation of a white officer— complete with buttons, stripes, belt and coattails.*

Declaration of Independence

When, in the midst of the thriving alien
Corn of congratulation for clever auspices
To spray out cruel politics like little birds
Set in rows, knocking them and breaking
The backs, just to suck out blood
Of complacency and dumb wistful resignation
Whose dumpy quality is force-fed inward
Against the natural flow of their actual
Energies all their lives, doubly dizzy
From wheezing through nostrils of boredom
On a vacation isle they fought for frantically
Only to ruin and poison artificially
With plastic clicking hands holding mule-like
Pills of false and clotted rest, *then* I
Get up much earlier than the rest, and smoke
Under creaking trees shocked by ice,
Lace of sunlight, glittering fir and snow,
Hours eating from this planet's tasty
Dwindling peace of mind.

United at First

United at first
ham and cheese fall apart and slip
        through my trembling hands

Just indoors and plenty hungry
from playing on the rough Pacific's shore
where it becomes very grainy and sort of deranged
with shattered fortress rocks and hopping surf
disappears in a second like breath escaping
at Mendocino on the high-strung edge of California

Fog brings visions

My mind is soaking wet but still works
overtime like my mouth
from looking at the protein
and melted green foam floating
on Pacific membrane far below

Come see this sandwich

Wiry Indian braves long ago
watch closely
as the sandwich is gobbled
by a lost Spaniard. They comment on it.
They get hungry, too
and start for the ambushed stranger
who backs away, "Doan touch me"
    "Stay clear"   "Watch out, my friends"

But this harried white man is falling asleep
        in a pouch of early morning sunlight
like a baby, soon forgetting
        the secrets of his craft. No more sandwiches.

Stage-hands now carry through the bleached eucalyptus
a huge plaster of Paris sandwich, spray-painted
bright red and green sliced tomatoes
and sprigs of parsley between the trees.
The sandwich is propped against the Spaniard's foot
        for him to meditate upon.

Come see this sandwich

And he "comes to see it"
        in his dreams. In his waking too.

    2.

A fortnight later: the besieged Moor
reaches the Great Salt Lake. Monstrously depressed
he takes his own life. Booths sell replicas of his spurs . . .

Things are going badly for the settlers and their wives

Some take to repairing old landscapes
others make hot soup from the gloom

One other
standing alone like a
lonesome pine at midnight
sings to a nervous pony and the moon
and his wife, his children
their friends and grade school teachers
and, via live recording, millions more

He's the same desperate Spaniard
            who's scratching at your door

     3.

By definition, Indians migrate and evolute
taking thousands of years
to do this . . . It's the whittling of a flute.
The separate tribes don't know each other
although they've heard stories
about a char-broiled elk steak across the Great Water
the great warm water
and bags of Wonder-Woman Tea

Orgiastic brew—

Now you're *really* hungry and
unwind a strip of dried buffalo
nickels, stored in plugs of virgin American snow

Maiden snowfall, storms of the young.
Lovely changes of light and texture
on faultless winter mornings, time to move on . . .

Watch you change from nymph to mother in seconds flat
Giving birth on the road, juggling and shaking

Spots and deep red stars appear before your eyes

Visions of nostalgic wonder

Toothpaste

Carrots

Pork chops

Ajax

Out the remote-controlled
doors of a supermarket, where are you? . . .
Oh yes, there's your soul brother's Chevrolet,
and taking your soul sister's underpass
you pull up at a front door just in time
to see it burn, lighting up a marathon
of bodies wrapped in flame-colored clothing
galloping across the lawn toward where you sit
revving up the motor and releasing a sigh
as your eyes glass over

4.

Glass over, twin instruments of all vision
filling past its brim
                a masonite Dixie cup
on the inventor's nerve-ridden worktable.
Nearby, a foam-induced portrait of his daughter,
some lucite toy dreamers, and a thought-pencil
with built-in spurt control . . . The inventor is madly successful
but too obsessed to live in peace
"Mystery stuffs its aces up my sleeve," he sings
to himself, "without even saying *please*"

Shedding a cough, he pulls himself
to valley-view window . . . Happy window of carefree dreams.
"What do I see," he muses in childlike delicate reverie—
"I see a human being stalking through trees at me"

It's the mailman! He has the day's circulars
in his buff leather pouch, a cigarette at his lip,
a rip in his pants just above the knee.
His name is Albert. His friends call him Albert.

But the inventor simply calls him over
asks for mail, gets it, and pauses
wondering if he can say anything to
                    awaken this poor fellow
from years of barren slumber in yesterday's forests.

The inventor, however, is much too condescending
to give sweet advice, and a mailman
is precisely what Albert wants and needs to be.
The two men part company after exchanging a few last words
and a promise made to meet upon the morrow.

Upon the morrow sits a televised bird
united at first, then it comes apart
so it can be packed & shipped in wings and legs
to the inventor: he has it now, but will he make it chirp?

The Booklets

"I can't believe it sometimes when I look in the mirror"

You kept saying this, or rather
the Buddha kept saying it
or so you thought—

Someone was saying it
while meanwhile in the dining room
six orphans autographed a basketball
and rolled it out the door

Outside it was raining hard, but it was also
really very beautiful, so beautiful in fact
people passing by
        began passing out on the grass
leaving their umbrellas and portfolios
and booklets of favorite sayings with the orphans
who collected all this and burned it in the bathtub
returning to the ones passed out on the grass

Pretty soon it stopped raining. People woke up,
stretching and popping their joints. They prowled around
greeting each other and stopped sometimes
to shoot the breeze, and sometimes to make love,
but always keeping at least one eye on the sky—
and the weaker ones yearned for their booklets.

Strolling with the Adults

We walked, bickering, out of the distant past
           and up an asphalt turnpike
But they were the same thing, a screen over which

Automobiles owned and operated by daydreams rolled
           in a steady stream—hundreds of millions
Riding toward what, for scholars, is the all-necessary,
Compelled by the blazing sunlight of tradition
To take frequent trips through pigeon-holes:
It is not religion, not amusing, not
Wise. This they do with a confident insolence that sprouts
From the stupendous index to all indexes . . .

Stopping near toll booths to eat we talked instead
           until stupor about our losing teeth
Overwhelmed us, along with the rest of the teeth
Of the entire present adult population
On earth—one mouth must account for them all.

And, like that mouth,
Any genuine reality is an infinite
           which passes all understanding and yet
Admits of being directly and, in some way, totally
           hungry:
Large quantities of sliced baloney
And adrenalin, blood sugar and a vitamin deficiency,
Or beating themselves through a cerebral valve
Whose efficiency once had been knowledge
And bliss. That's why, in spite of its obvious wonders,
Some areas remain in the brain from which the probing occurred.

But the patient, who was under a local anaesthetic, finds
                    upon waking
That valid transcendental experiences are looked upon
                    with a lack of vitamin C, and pellagra, caused
By a shortage in the operating room and environment,
An environment still slick with rain but profoundly different
From that in which our forefathers passed their lives.

The Trumpets Are Coming

When the sound of someone clearing his throat
In the blind darkness of night and sky overhead
Makes the hair on my head
Stand up, then I stand up too.
I walk back inside myself and turn on the radio—
      Vexations, by Erik Satie.
I am cold. A door creaks open
But footsteps don't bring hot cocoa.
Instead they bring a bone, it is a dog
One more in a homogenized series of dogs
That look alike: dogs of the same breed
Look alike. But these dogs,

Not only are they different breeds,
They are not all of them
Dogs. Some are ghostly trumpets
You hear playing very faintly
Behind the music you were listening to
      originally.
You realize
The trumpets are coming
From another station
And you do your best to tune them out.

What America's Thinking

Words are free
Ants bigger than elephants
The dentists all drive Cadillacs now

Tonight is different
I'm the girl wearing the icepack
At six-thirty the blankets come hopping upstairs

Christmas has arrived early this year—June 3rd
Curious shifting of the stars
The stockbroker chewing on a small red cigar

Seagulls just won't remember us
Terraces of binding resonance
My fist at seventy miles an hour

This has nothing to do with having a house or a job
Does anything ever stand still?
This has nothing to do with wearing a watch

Americans unloading props and psychology invisibly
Concentric spheres of intuition
We stand up as a rule before leaving the room

Houses are built on solid ground
Trees grow daily naturally
Houseflies orient themselves mysteriously

People who have faces are individuals
Houseflies have one face and are collected
Dogs, cows and cats fall somewhere in between

Dogs: cows and cats underline our human size
The sizes bend as they change
The dogs jump up and lick the moon

In architecture, styles come and go
Architecture is part of an invisible cultural balloon
The baby releases the string

The television is just on
I am just on
The big dog's bright companion

Bob Robertson waits on deck
The corkscrew comes alive under the dining room rug
The Bronx creamery reflected in old Shoshone eyes

Transparent music, aboriginal patterns, biological too
Ice-age rhythms
But right here in this room

When you live in a house now you have a job
The men finish dinner and adjust their commemorative flags
They adjust their fortune cookies and paper napkins

Adjusting parched leaves in smoky piles means autumn
Adjusting the politics changes the temperature
The back door hisses smoothly, then it shuts

Today the man sees something absolutely new
Curtains of supersonic, pulsing flashes
The apple's view of Newton

Technicians tinker at home on rainy days in flannel shirts
The sun sifting through stainless steel mesh and grids
Technicians rarely get enough sun

Atoms are invisible but real
This isn't confusing, children grasp it with cries of joy
The electron microscope, little voices in the distance

The little voices gather together for speed
The atoms hurtle down a small red cigar
They spout into the room, showering the startled stockholders

Geography

I make my home in a state of mind
bordering on infancy
and, to the south, tenacity.
To the north rides mature
wisdom, that rides like a horse.
The horse.
To the west is love, careless love.
To the east is power.

You can't ever be too rash with an old machine.

What old machine?

Ripped out of my mind again
"Ripped out of my mind again"—
how many people have said that?
or how can people say that?
or how many people can say that?
Did . . . uh, did Guido Cavalcanti say that?
Did Roger the Bush say that?

Did "the bush" say that?
The irises?   The maples?
The arms?   The palmettos?

Did the Indians say that?
The Chinese?
The Braves?

*

I hold my piece
For a while and tell you something

*

How many men
and women did you say that would make?

How many men and women did
you say that would make?

How many men would you say
what that meant?

Did you say something?
Did you say something?

*

I can hear the disembodied populace in the trees
Blowing their golden horns and pieces
Bounce their music across the grass
Into my EAR

Not Van Gogh ear, just me

What is that supposed to mean?
What is that supposed to mean?

*

We all have bodies!

Faces!

We all have names!

*

Do we all have places?
Do we all have places?

     I have place, I think
it's home, in a state of mind
bordering on fantasy and, to the south,
insistency. To the north is manure

but we avoid that like a horse
galloping west, where we see love
where we hear and see love, where we
touch and hear and see love.

To the east lies power. Amphetamine.

*

I feel so happy now!
I feel so great now!

Now I keep feeling it!
Now I keep on feeling!

Now I don't feel it so much

Now I don't feel that way anymore
Now I don't feel that way anymore

Now I don't care
Now I just don't care anymore

Who gives a fuck now
Who gives a fuck anyway

Now I don't give a fuck
Now I don't know

Now it sounds pretty heavy
Now it's getting very heavy

Now it's horrible
Really horrible

Now that's funny
Now that sounds funny
Now that's pretty funny

Now that sounds pretty funny

Now that's great!
No, really, that's really great!
Really incredible!
That's just fucking amazing!
That's so amazing!

I can't believe it!

I feel so happy now!

So great!

*

I found out
What geography means:
    it doesn't mean
      jigsaw colored shapes
   of the different states:
Arizona,   New York,   Etcetera

It means where I make myself space

*

I make myself space
where I make my time

I make my time in a state
of strange mess bordering on ecstasy
and, to the south, lunacy.
To the north snores calm maturity
Calm serenity that handles himself
like a horse.
        The right horse.
The west is relative, like love
unbelievably stubborn rays of careless love
sun of love that agitates you
and in a moment
for just a moment
innocent and melancholy bleeding heart.

In the east rumbles power.
The sweet machine. Amphetamine.

An old man.

*

If you ever change your mind
About leaving it all behind
Remember
Remember

No geography

     Me
   You and me
Him and her and them, too
    And you
          and me, too

I'll take you along
I'll take you along with me
I'll take you along with me

Let's go
Let's go

      Where's that?
      Where's that?

         *

Let's go to Colorado!

    Let's go to Kyoto!

Let's go to the sofa!
    The big leather sofa!

Let's go to the pouch!
Let's go to the pouch!

The animals in the pouch!

Listen to the vitamins maneuvering!

Cake your head in rock!
Cake your head in granite rock!

Let's go to New York!

*

Now, what is New York?
Now, what is New York?

What could be New York?

Could that be where I was
before I came here
to hear the horns of micro-organ animation
blown thru the entirety of magnetic
situations here, in a state of mind
bordering on all the ages and speeds

I can ever have—

Is that what the old girls called karma?
Is that what the old girls called karma?

*

And that brings me hovering above the south
where I see, spread out below me
my tenacity. To the north it's calmer
and clear, exactly like a horse trotting
back and forth across his own body.
That's wisdom.

To the west is careless love.

And in the east
        complicated and selfish
     and rude
              is power.
Power.

Six Hot Biscuits

1. You give him the money. He looks at you with a crooked smile on his face and gives it back. "I got the money already," he says. "I don't need from you."

2. You're inside a clam stand . . . And I mean *inside*—underneath the white wooden counter, down on your knees in the grass. On top of you, someone else is selling clams to someone else. You can feel the blue clouds sailing by overhead. You're dizzy from the smell of fresh white paint.

3. Denmark. A shakiness in the trees by the roadside fried potato stand. A cool summer day in Jutland. Two German boys wearing lederhosen alight from iron bikes. They are hawk-faced.

4. Thomas M. Disch approaches you unexpectedly on the quais of Paris, clutching a stack of polychrome postcards of Egypt—the Great Sphinx and Cheops Pyramid, groups of villagers wading up the Nile, etc. He insists that you take them home with you and "experience them." He is dressed in a squash-yellow polo shirt with white piping, short-sleeved, under a wash-and-dry raincoat. His feet are shod in hush puppies. "I'm looking forward very much to seeing you while you're in Paris," he says and then walks off without leaving you his address.

5. The good man, who lives upstairs in Apt. 8 . . . He climbs the stairs each night with a good-natured hello in his heart. He greets his two small children with a glad and complete serene voice of utter contentment. He has found out life's secret, and he is truly grateful. His wife is waiting for him at the top of the stairs. Holding a soup spoon in her left hand, she cradles two infants with her right, and radiates light like a polynesian hole card. Looking at them as he ascends the stairs, he decides he'll defend them with his life, if he has to.

6. You turn on the radio, hoping to hear music. Instead you hear someone saying, "We make our own, and we make it better than anyone else." An exotic northern tune goes through your ears, like a shooting star, but you can't really hear it because it's in your head. You reach over and turn off the radio. Someone is walking up and down the stairs out in the hall. "Out in the hallway!" someone shouts. Someone else is rattling keys. You are in the Big City. You have come from somewhere else and rented a room, or two rooms, and you have stayed. For seven years now you have stayed.

Triplets

Exaggerated lives, phony body postures, overblown gestures
Flashy plastic clothes, subliminal packaging, no architecture
Cosmetic patina covering the face, neck and hands

Averted glances, city block survival, celery stalks at midnight
Dogshit, stunted sycamores, unisex block and tackle
Inverted weather front, stagnant airshaft, walleyed abdication

Politics, art, artificial beef and monster injected chicken
Aerosol junkies spray themselves illusory jellied youth product
Trash 14th St., vinyl nazi Madison, Plymouth Rock retirement village

Sensory deprivation, smokescreen social causes, "What about me?"
Lowest common denominator, subway to nowhere, quaint souvlaki
People turning into pullets, distributor caps, jack hammers

The Sidewalk

The sidewalk never changes. The street
Always changes. It changes my feet—
On the outside of this old apartment wall
Street violence and harsh dark speech
The heartless gunning of an idiot's engine
His numberless swift cars
That spew out noise like rubble down the street
Cutting between the two great academic lines of heat
The positive and negative poles
Of the sidewalks, always too hard
For the defeated pairs and pairs and pairs of feet

These feet are gobbled down dreamily by Time
Who is Chronos by Goya and
One of the really Big Boys—
He swerves across the sidewalk at me for a dime
As I leap outside and hit the street

A Stretch of City Street

The most secret grief-struck noise precedes and now
                    surrounds me here
Where a random idiot Armenian descended child
Beats a console TV with a frozen side of beef
Like a chili pepper colony struck by herds of waxen sheep.
He joys to bequeath, though sight unseen, to me
Toys that squirt out lack of sleep. A life-sized tuba
You might want to turn around and murder his noise with, by
Clamping him down to the pavement with your tuba from above:
He is just a child, but this is never love.
And he's joined by—well, by how many more?
They must think of themselves as characters out of Melville
Because, clop clop clop . . . the rainy romantic street
Intrudes like a tear-jerker into their bottomless idio-
                    syncrasies:
Dunks his doughnut just *thus*, combs out her beard exclusively
Thusly, prefers (in fact insists) to have his *Post* delivered
Just at the highly personal, obviously obscure moment
When slow screeching giddy gypsies break for lunch
Allowing the street a rare half hour of silence . . .
What is it berates us like a lunch of rubber hamburger?
What is it makes the plastic creep?

Liberty Bells

The liberty bells are ringing

The people pour down from their scallop-shell rooms

To stride excitedly among each other

Distracted and intense, seemingly elated

But fiercely aimless, up & down the streets

Move Over Dick Gallup

Dignified poverty is an exciting condition
About like falling off a log
Into a tarpit of euthanasia
But it has its bright side, too—at least
We won't have to be screwing people to the wall
From nine to five, collecting alimony from a blind pig.
And it lets us use our energies for other things
If we will.
Driving a cab, for instance.
How exhilarating it is for me
On this, the night before I take the final step
Toward obtaining my hack license,
How fabulous it is for me to anticipate
Driving up and down these legendary streets
Hunched forward, like the rest, behind the wheel
But with a plastic fever shield between me and them
Protecting me from their mad quarantine
As they lead the way from the rear.

For Them

For them the Arctic is the image, a touch of eternity
The perpetual coming on of Winter
The milk's been in the icebox for three weeks now
It still *looks* white but it tastes kind of grey
Drifting away here on the Alex Quinn Show
"Librium 25 mg. has usually been found to provide
Dependable control of severe anxiety, affording
Basic Support as an adjunct to counsel and reassurance."
Polyrhythmically metamorphosed illuminated ceilings.
I stare up at the ceiling and easily can see
There's gonna be a rumble up in Paradise tonite.
But I no longer believe the story that is commonly told.
The story goes that I stood up among them in the endless
American meeting hall and yelled, "You goddamn idiots!
Why don't you just shape up!"
Then my heart grew huge and started beating madly
My eyes wildly spilled out onto the street
And I became one of them. Yes, I became that which
I most did not wish to become.
For during their stages of development
All things appear under forms
Opposite to those that they finally present.
This is an ancient doctrine.
I am thirty-one years old.
The newspapers tell me there's a revival of Charles Ives
Going on now, and I have to laugh:
What about the immense SMILE button, pal,
Whose rusty pin jabbed into your heart adds its color to your fate?
How's it feel to survive on a diet of newsprint and chickenshit?
They must be drugging 'em like pillars of salt up in Paradise tonite.
Paradise, whose baggy white clouds and thin green sky

29

The newspapers utterly fail to notice. Silly newspapers.
And the lingering image of the soft bowling-green Connecticut garden
That spawned Charles Ives
In a summertime in which many flowers bloom
Is actually the exact mirror image of the Arctic
Where the taxis are waiting in their long white room.
They start up all over again every morning
Without a single word . . . Except that it says here
An Army spokesman could not respond tonite
About reported plans to manufacture "ton quantities"
Of VX, an odorless, colorless compound
That attacks the nervous system
When inhaled or absorbed through the skin.
A quart jar of VX allegedly contains
"Several million lethal doses," the aide said.
The heart swoons while the head just fades away.
And if, as Goethe said, architecture is frozen music
Then it sounds today as if a pack of rats
Is slowly being tortured to death.
Let me make this as clear as possible:
The metal door downstairs slams and the building vibrates
With the sound of the one subway going by
And the sound of the other subway being built . . .
Yes, a new subway is being built for them.
It will take nineteen years and cost 4 billion dollars
And by the time it opens all of them will be gone,
All for whom it's being built will have vanished from the streets
    forever.
They will have surfaced by then somewhere deep inside the Arctic Circle
Carrying with them an entirely different, new set of needs
Primary among which will be the overwhelming need for a nice
    hot drink
And a fire, and a friend.

What's the Problem Here?

Why is it sometimes
I feel good
Sometimes I feel bad
And the times I don't feel at all

Times I don't feel at all drift—
I can't even say this—
Drift past my window
Because the window in this poem
Is in this poem
But hold it, a second
Hold it
Just hold it

*

I don't know, can't remember who told me
Human energy's in-depth-charge
The earth's treasures above
And beyond, also below, behind, above the earth
Inside the arm of the right arm raised
That holds this surface
Inside the great winter sausage I used to love
Cooking up on icy, helpless nights—
Just you and me and Goose
Pecking around and rolling the golden egg
We kept falling asleep

O river
Play me that river song again

Wash me with your buckets
Hanging from the ears of your banks

*

Whereas sometimes on a hot & dusty night
I really love to watch you
Hanging out of my shirt

Your body stares at me and says, "Who are you?"

Which is what I love

*

I remember, though
You don't have to tell me
I forget
But then I tell you anyway
"How could you ever forget?"

But Lester remembers, he disappeared
In Manila in the year 1932

He was a rare person

My aunt, who was very beautiful
And strange
And who nobody in our family ever really liked
Used to spend hours with me
Cocking me her melancholy head across the colors
In some kind of living room
Telling me about Lester, how she had followed him

To the ends of the earth
In the early thirties
To Manila
Where he died, or actually
I can't say that because he just disappeared—

"Yama yama yama," he said,
"I'm going to merge with the pillars
Beyond x-number of coconut palms
And Pacific situations here, because you see
This situation is indefinitely extensible—
They are real, the streets and towns and windows
Through which the faces you see
As you walk along are looking"

Outside

1.

No, I *don't* feel like going to see
Night of the Living Dead—I feel like
I've seen that movie before
And that movies on the whole is all I've
                    ever seen!

A coin of spotlight travels the kitchen wall
(I'm sure you've seen that coin before)
And I'm sure you can see a little man tuxedo
                    top hat, running
To keep up with it: that little man
Is my contribution to the great movie-going
                    public
That horde I feel I know so well
But not tonite. Tonite
The stars are out, so cheap
So sharp
They sting me with their absence, and I understand:

            "All time goes fast in
            The better to see back out again"

—Did you know that?

2.

I step outside and it's like I've lost control
Not that I haven't been here before, but
Another, greater problem is loosening my fillings
                    right now, and I cry out—

—Is that the window, old white mother, a rattlin?
Is that the real field and stream out there?
Is that the old black mare a snortin?
                    Why then, here
                we all are again!
Isn't that something? All of us back here
Together again, just like Noah's Ark?
I can hardly believe it. In fact,
            I don't believe it.

But *it* doesn't care what I believe, *it*
                doesn't need me, it goes right back
Outside again, oblivious to what I might want
Or feel—"Have you sent the invitations yet
            to Mrs. Spiegelmann?" it whispers haughtily
And goes back outside again, just like it used to be
                (Remember?)
With the rest of us still here inside.
We're in here and *it's* out there, and I'll
            be darned again.

3.

. . . Well in that case, I'm going back outside.
Nothing can stop me!
                    Listen!
Is that the window, old white mother, a rattlin?
Is that the old black mare a shakin?
            Why, I thought
She been standing there shakin for nigh on
            two million years!
I bet she can't even read or write!
            (O my goodness)

35

Then I got a funny feeling: I thought
—Was my head, all that time, still in my ear?
For so many hundreds of thousands of years?

4.

I can't go on

A contract streaming

Down from the sky

How can I sign a contract made of water? . . .

Where's my steam bag?

Where's my otter?

5.

. . . Now it's like it was before.
Just like it was before: every hair and apple
in its place.
All the fruits and flowers, airborne aviators
swamps and ticks and bees, houses and raisins
and trees, rolling gently watercolor
Like a page from a baby coloring book

"I can hardly wait to take a look"

Streaming, streaming

Days and weeks and months go by

6.

Tears of God, etc., water our garden
Until the bulls come out and roll their marbles
                    in the rain

—A simple movement I live to see but not explain.

Mankind Poem

Bacon and eggs are old, old
It's seven a.m.
I'm outside hopping with the blackbirds
    in the field and I'm cold—
Bring my breakfast plate, God, into the eastern sky
Nourish me and give me life, and give me coffee too

Stupefied Aborigines

Stupefied aborigines
Who study for the first time
The sentient earlobes
That hang suspended from no ears at all
Are no more stupefied than I was
Upon first being folded into
And then hopelessly knowing
This whole world

The Wind

The wind
Blows everything away
Including love
Including hate
In waves the wind
Can you hear it calling
Can you hear the wind call your name?

Poem ("Distance makes the heart . . .")

Distance makes the heart grow weirder
Butterfly struck by cedar waxwing shadow

Furniture Music

Throughout the Golden Age, throughout all of this—this—*prancing*, the tables and chairs in our bright clean apartment remain still. A confident, cool silver to offset our raucous gold. Such quiet, infinitely generous vibrations rise from the furniture and work their way across our faces.

Do you remember? Was it in San Francisco? That weekday so long ago? A powdery, brushed-aluminum '40's feeling to the light? Because of the windows? The frosted glass parallelograms framed by handsome sleek strips of aluminum? The flat brass railings that ran like ribbons up the concrete steps outside? Was it too early in the morning to be going to the store? Were we waiting for the store to open?

But the door was open, wasn't it; children were playing in the yard below. In fact, a thousand children ran howling and screaming up and down, up and down the yard below. So much noise they made! We wondered why, exactly. Why? Why do children make so much noise? But an ancient person was in the backyard, too, a teacher, quietly and sagely feeding instructions and structuring the squishy energy of the breathless children.

Did the children all suddenly notice we were looking down at them? Did they look up and see us? Huh?

The tables and chairs lean forward: they want to know the answer— they act as if they have a *right* to know. Proudly they take their places amid waves of rich, hushed expectancy and whipped cream. The rugs and lamps and pillows expect an answer, too. They lean forward infinitely, together with the chairs. Time passes so outstandingly. The sun strikes out across the floor with a high yellow hand.

"*People* are the only sun!" the tables and chairs seem to say—they love us so.

Streets & Sheets

The last great continental glacier melted away less than 10,000 years ago.

Great sheets of ice change the weather. When the front of a glacier stood in Milwaukee, it must have been bitterly cold in Chicago.

I've been to Chicago . . . Although it wasn't particularly cold there I ran screaming silently in comical fear and revulsion all the way to the airport, where I caught the first plane out. It was the endless repetition of row houses, the never-ending procession of empty brick streets, that brought out my abrupt longing for emigration.

I see now that if I had been a temperate-climate herbivore back then before the last ice age, the ice sheets certainly would have inspired trouble in my heart long before the first sheet ever became visible . . . One day I would have raised my head from the grass I was eating and sadly sensed what I never before could have seen: rows and rows of houses that crept down from an unknown north until they surrounded me.

The streets of Chicago live on in my memory as more than enough of a suffocating element I was lucky to shake off by sprouting wings. The sheets lie back there in Chicago too: they are sleeping now but everyone knows that soon they'll be awake.

The Sacred Life of the Future

The sacred life of the future
Will be personally architectural and more
Finely spaced and carefully tuned than ours.
And when something new finally does
Come to replace it, we'll be left
With more than the tall shiny "Go fuck
Yourself, buddy" of today.
In the future, fine.
In the past, not so good.
At present, it's paradise.
Life inside the rim of a sexual tin can.
I lift two fingers and it's a man.
The fingers walk and it's a woman.
In the future such constellations
Will all become ingredients
Dissolved in the space between each other
Instead of from on high, as it is today, in outer space
Pounding the other person into oblivion
With a big white rubber foot.

Men Waiting for Geese

Time flies
in circles:
the revolution
of the earth
around think
what else besides
the sun

*

A wheel is rolling
on the frost
david show

I know
I know

*

Listening
Listening
What's that
someone outside?
man falling over inside?

*

A man in the potato fields
adjusting his decoys
about 200 yards away from me

45

He's set out 15 or 16
huge black and grey goose decoys
now there's another one

Two men now, loading their rifles
I can't believe it!
they crouch down around behind a bale of hay
waiting.

*

Waiting for what?

Geese?

Men waiting for geese?

True Story

What an old man
from Lima, Ohio told me once
when I asked him
if I'd come to the right person
around Lima for directions—
"I been struck by lightning, son,
    I don't know nothing"

Thanksgiving

I bought the Maverick last year and my wife
And I are still real happy about it

Moon Chevrolet

Moon Chevrolet Times
Square, 1942

. . .

Moon Chevrolet Times
Square, 1945

. . .

Moon Chevrolet Times
Square, 1946

. . .

Moon Chevrolet Times
Square, 1951

Ninth Symphony

I put on my socks: the men in the next room put on their socks. I put on my coat: the men in the next room take off their hats. I loosen my shoes: they burn their socks. I take off my shoes: they cannot do this.

I rip my scarf: they burn their shoes. I slip on my leather vest: the girls in the next room roll their bracelets, their graduation bracelets, and move up a flight. On the second floor the girls are taking off their harmonicas. The elephants are rising on their hind legs: they are trained.

I am going out for a soda. I am going out for a piece of bread. Leave the door open for me. Tell the men to put on their coats: I am hungry. Tell the men to shine their shoes.

Tell the two women to brush their wigs. They should clean their coats. Tell them to sponge their furs. They should eat something soon: they're going to be hungry when there's no more food.

Tell the other three women to buckle their helmets. Tell the boys to hurry. Tell the men to hurry: I am tired of waiting.

Strange Days Ahead

Oceanic push-ups

Flavored green thumbprints

The moon many times seven

Rollo mine flavored sweep-o-mints

The chicken gun

Flame-o-sweeps

Target palms sweeping up oceanic lanes

Target flipper

Days I surround my lanes with

The flipper in the green filler

State of filtered ripple go way

Nah go way

Ripple and run

Oceanic freshness

Oceanic tank

Oceanic leaves blowing

Why Is Space

Why is space
the outside
or outer,
"visible"
side of time?

We are time caps, that much I know
And the surface of the ball is space—

The world of space, the external world—
and the air inside is time?

Change is time, I know—
but is space?

Then why is space always blue?
Why is outer space black?

Sunday Afternoon

It's dark jerseys defending for Motor City
The 100,000,000 spectators break down
Into their component parts of sunglasses—
Magic circles of frenzy, dark doughnuts glazed
With speed, circles of muscle that sail back and forth
Left-right, left-right
Feeding themselves to the afternoon television
Inside an aquarium of perpetual grey light:

This is a professional football game,
So now the muscles contract and expand nonsensically—
What a sight!—And to see that, to actually hear
And see a criminal idiot address a joint session
Of Congress, circles of muscle throbbing
In unison—Can you understand what that kind of thing
Does to me? It drives me further and further up the wall
Of the stadium, where I look back down and see
The classical, sad football players collide
In flat ballet shoes on the astroturf.

Baby Blue Eyes

It's like this: a doormat
Then a door
Then the doormat
Outside the dog house
Housing the dog that rambles rhetorically there
"Bow wow wow" he says, inviting you in
And you caca sweetly, like the dog
And you do go in
And sit yourself down
Alongside the world-famous "Rubber Bone"

Soon you're surrounded by dogs
Finite sizes, shapes and colors of dogs
So many smelly old dumb dogs
Then you look closer, and harder, and you see
The dogs are regarding you with baby blue eyes
Instamatic and true eyes, intense and remarkable too
Blue skies too, and scuddy yellow strips of cloud
Whole placid landscapes and troubled cities that somehow
Personally come to seek you out
From inside dozens of baby blue eyes—
Remarkable marmalade, wouldn't you say?

    2.

And that's not the half of it:
The other half's plugging away too,
Cats
Whose huge, complicated drippy hearts
Are ruled by the pounding waves of their emotions
That come gurgling all over you like a big baby
Driving a runaway station wagon

And the gas station attendants for that matter, too
Who lope up and peer in at you as you wait for gas:
Then they leave, and so do you
Though it wasn't their gas but their eyes
                that made you leave.

3.

"Adhere!" calls the marmalade
"Intense!" cry out the eyes
And the lower half that's smoked too much
Weeps forever
While the upper half grits some upper teeth
And like a helpmate sees it through
Every evening of every life

Yes, you have many lives
Many costumes and parts of costumes
Like this funny meringue office building
Or this completely out-of-whack dog brush . . .
Unfortunately, they're all adhering to your body
At once, like marmalade, making
The whole chaotic drama so suspenseful
It grabs for your heart like the baby blue eyes
Of dogs that never stop

The Big Picture

In the big picture, I see man
as hot potato
      passed on to the hands of woman
who is joined to the mammals on the wheel of life
by her feet—I see
many feet walking, and some men running
and the feet are well-formed
      and marvellous to behold

And the shoes the men wear
      prod and investigate
and kick the sleeping dog that lies
at the foot of woman—and the dog awakes
and bites the man, & if he's more than a man
      he bites back

Unmasked at Last

Giant cobwebs are strung across my living room
They snare gifts thrown at me by neighbors
      and friends
      for my children—
Yes, I have eighty-six children and I live
      off the gifts people give them . . .

Now that we know who I am
      we can proceed

To who *you* are, you who say:
  "He's like that, can't help it!
But what about US?"

             *

Many boxes box in bursting men
Whose lives are the streets
Between those boxes and back again
And although I am alive too
Mine is a shadow box
And you are my sun,
"You"

             *

. . . the old people, carving
      peach-pit villages
            by candlelight . . .

             *

Lucid intervals
Of screw-loose transcendence
Fewer each year

While your everyday self
Sits at the kitchen table
Pounding its fists and wailing
"Give me more food!

*

I'm ready now

 I try anything: to eat the stately worms
Of Melanesia, even, don't bother me

Latin cribs, Chinese checkers, gnomes of Zurich—
  I couldn't care less

The view from the bridge of the giant bagel works
  breaks Spinoza's lenses

As in a seagull or anything else, the massive speedy

 Sky-Wall-Man factor:

The man is loading and tamping down his pipe now

 Now he lights it
 And *nogga he ga ligga*
 Nogga he ga ligga

*

"Squirt, squirt"
goes the ten o'clock news
and "squirt, squirt" goes my heart

*

"In the absence
of external excitations
coming through
the natural end organs,
perception systems
maintain this activity
all on their own . . ."

*

"I have no sense of history!"
   said the rhododendron to the crazed
dope fiend.

*

Then came the legions of indignant snowballs
Thrown at police moving in vans to maintain order
Solidified by the dental tartar of respect
For wasp squads striking at the tender places
Of history, again
For a final roundup and identity check
   Of the manipulated millions:

"Where were you born?"
"How do you live?"
"What would you like for breakfast?" etc.

*

The afternoon sun creeping up the carpet

It's cheaper for you to become a statistic
Than it is to remain alone,
Go where and when you want to go.
I'm not kidding you, buddy.
Cheaper to go for 21 days
Than just to go.

They returned my package
Because I hadn't used the zip code

My package full of sun . . .

*

A blackeye today for the administration of grassland justice
Black fins guide the retreating Cadillacs
That swallow up red lights in heavy rain
Taillights behind the eyeballs of the men
Their secret, plodding affliction
Lodged directly below the nose

It's not a big affliction, though—
The size of a TV screen

*

. . . now Big Mouth opens—

a fistful of dollars—

I won't let it happen, though

here in your dollar

where you wait to tuck me in—

The Raven Reigns!

Wolf

Claw and

Plastic Bucket—

A still life gives you the right to fuck it

*

Museum whose doors are the sparkling eyelid's toothbrush

Museum of History, insufferable hallucination of self-pride's

big mitts—

What good is your red carpet to me now?

Where we scrub and polish, and on watery knees we pray—

O Lord, Make Your
House Fall Down—
Let all your chairs and tables run free!

*

The chairs turn their chairs to the wall and say:

Clouds, you give me the best idea

Spooky Mozart loggia leaning down
out of the clean white wallboard walls
holding big blue clouds

Who is sitting up there?

Who's listening?

*

Much time passes: a bird

on wheels

*

Another bird perches on your hand
Two more land on your lips
Sing-song little brothers
Who've had their dinner on a single speck
of technicolor grain
Which you won't ever see again

Speck this and speck that
　　but you'll never see *that* bird again
Because now you go funny
And set your controls for the heart of the sun

　　　　　　　*

(Music is stately, lovely music.
Rolls of wallpaper, rolls of bliss.
The stately, worthy music of the *Nogga Ligga*.)

Hard to Please

Unstable life forms
Yield dry, fiery karma

Shouts a desperate voice
Crooning from dizzy cartoon rocks

Frenzied bellow of the puzzled mastodons
Sunk up to their holsters in dollar bills

Leaving chaos behind and watching
The *Motel Manager's Training School* ad

Now on TV
MU 7-3500

Test patterns on the screen
Time for bed

The Marine Band playing stars
And stripes forever, the flag is rippling

In a perfect & up immortal breeze
Five feet from your nose but miles
            and miles away through the windy tube

Garden City Jitters

I truly wish the righteous monkey
Konk your hair in airless
Hide your baby atlas under the stands
To camouflage remote emotions, invading Mineola—click.
The monkey that bounds head-first down 1st. St.
That stands you on your hands—click,
So you can see in your despair that what in 1959
Was fields and marshes, coves and inlets
Is now where the foolish rows of houses stand

It Can't Be True

That we belong to one of the last generations
To see an uncontaminated sky
And walk through enough forest
Stretching for hundreds of square miles
Uncharted and completely surrounded by itself
Holding us because being there
Is a real surprise, vast and everyday
And not just the unspoiled tip
Of an island fenced off by the gov't.
For one brief, clumsy weekend
Fucking away from the glare of the city's
Shiny hallucination

43 Cents a Quart

Standing in line at the bank: what if this
Were on TV? What if we were all on mescalin?

The bank is made astounding, ineffable, inexorable
By the people who fill it
So mysterious
In their old-man overcoats
Or a squad of olive-drab sideburn otherness
And plumbers, deliverymen and "students" too
They're too much
Me too

An idle afternoon lady goes by
Her hair has been lacquered and sprayed
And makes her head (she's under five feet tall)
Look like a cabbage dipped in gold paint
Floating in the air ten inches from my stomach
Thank God my stomach doesn't have windows!

We're all standing in this line
Everyone looks so silly
Me too!
Riveted to the particular decimal track we're on
And knowing it, too

And the tellers, the bank guards
And supervisors
And then, off by themselves
On their pitifully "junior-exec" square
                    of special drab-gold carpet
Sit the two "officers"
The men whose simple initials on the back of your check
Can mean so much: 43 cents a quart

City Voices

"Shut up"
say the voices
from the street
as they retreat—
city voices, so
it's trick retreat.
Now a truck
and cabs go by.
Other voices fill the sky.

"Mother" shouts her mother.
Going to bind
her first mother
with yet another.
She's that down,
to be below there
beating on her other mother.

White noise
city garbage truck
growl and disembodied process grease
of garbage greeted and accepted
then squashed, reduced, pressed—

It must be money that tempts
the garbage to submit to this.

"Shut up, mother"
Louder, louder
"I'll send you down
        and find another"
Terrific strain, sudden silence—
Cans, meat, hands, retreat.

The Good Humor Men

Where ignorant armies clash by night

a Good Humor Man

flies to pieces

Speed

was his undoing

I am angry.
You are here.
She is gone.

We have problems.
You disappear.
All is well.

Well-meant, and proud of it

2.

The day before: a mailman
tripped out while delivering parcels
to the following address:

228 Lovesick Rd.
Sky Demeanor
Pot Luck, Crazy About
Nevada   66218

Where I hang my hat and knees

and burn my shoes

is where I hear you laughing

or do I hear you smiling

and eager, until snuffs out the Light.

3.

Your body and mine make three.

It is night. Somewhere
a star is born, and somewhere the band is playing to a worldwide con-
gregation of machinists, cowgirls, and vocational high schools. Going
extra-heavy on the doughnuts and beer. Political oblivion, confusion
and nirvana. Vertigo and stretches of blank tape occasionally in the
morning. Tiger lilies catapult into The Oxygen Tent, shaking their
heads. A breast falls to the ground (earth). A man falls to one knee,
afterwards. He is

smoking with fervor

the longest cigarette in the world (his world) . . .

a four-dimensional box

of four dejected lox

mailed to the following address:

Coaster
c/o Speed Coaster
23 Poster D.C.
Skit   41478

Act One taking place
in the glandular pinwheel of Sun & Stars
& Cartwheels that spin
across the outer space
of your self-conscious face

Act Two

and panes of light ignite the sandman
stumbling across your pillows
thru grains of love and morphine

The ocean pounding at your feet like a disembodied heart . . .

4.

Submarines and tight blue jeans
are the same size to a disillusioned sailor

but only up to a point, past which

you go on reading

and the bread goes on rising—

three smiling astronauts
sitting on its upper crust.

It has reached the moon now

And the elders are crying in their beer:

Swallows fly out of their mouths, for it
is dusk. Day is done. The bats avoid each other
as they sail into the belfry
        for a final multi-layered evening meal—
The dry cereal is for the animals and servants.
        The oatmeal is for real.

*   *   *

CODA

The underpants finally come to rest on the floor.

The girl is inspired, her frenzied fingers

Racing across the oily keys

Of an electric baby grand. Who else

is listening?

Are the good humor men listening?

Dinner Music

"You must be starving," said the rat-catcher as he bent down and swept at some more rats with his reinforced butterfly net. I was there because we needed two more rats for dinner: we were expecting guests.

"You don't have to worry," he added. "If you lose one then you can use one chopstick and one ballpoint pen instead, you don't need two chopsticks." He lunged toward an especially plump Norway rat cowering in the corner. It was disgusting.

*

"Flgrp."

"Yeah, right . . . you think these lemons are real? Well, they *are* real. Ha ha." He stood, gazing in rapture at the lemons.

*

The sound of one chopstick eating: who cannot hear it?

*

. . .You see,

Long ago when the spirit and the belly were one, people used chopsticks to walk with. Not only in China, but all over . . . They said, "Well, I go now," and they hopped up on their chopsticks and disappeared down prehistoric chopstick-paths, their delicate ancestral chopstick-tracks imprinted in the ancient grasslands . . .

Futhermore, they ate most of their meals with microscopic versions of these chopsticks, which they called "knives and forks."—I know what a horrible joke that sounds like, but it's been substantiated conclusively that what prehistoric people called their miniature chopsticks was almost exactly what we call our chops and sticks: "nives" and "fokes."

However, the spoon was unknown to them. The spoon as such made its entrance on the historical scene four thousand and seven cardboard cartons later, when Lord Spoon stopped mid-way on his annual pilgrimage to Canterbury Cathedral and asked his aide-de-camp for a spoon. "But I have never heard of a spoon," the man replied. "Well, now you have," said Lord Spoon with a laugh: "Because I am that spoon!"

*

The shrimps turn red when you cook them, but actually they are grey. They taste so delicious. Personally I prefer chopsticks.

*

The chromatic fantasy and fugue goes on and on, and meanwhile the annual quota for wheat and barley is not being met! The Central Committee is furious!

*

A ghost with a 10-inch switchblade

Is stealing up behind you—

Look out!

He'll stab you right in the back!

—But, no, maybe he won't do that after all . . . Now that I've tuned in the set a little more clearly and wiped my glasses I see that in truth he's quite docile and contented, that ghost, munching away at his bowl of phantom rice and beans with his single ivory chopstick.

74

Or is that a ballpoint pen?

(He's much stranger than a ghost, after all . . .)

*

"Cirrhosis of the fantasy" was what the doctors called it, but I knew what their fancy terminology boiled down to in the end: more chopsticks.

*

Pass me the chopsticks, please. Thanks.

Listen to them splinter as I eat them. I want to eat all of them and I'm *going* to eat all of them. They taste so good, washed down with a few ballpoint pens.

*

Now I'm absolutely stuffed. I can't eat anymore. I sit back in my easychair and contemplate the shrimps:
"If carrots were chopsticks, what were shrimps?" I ask no one in particular, in a nice after-dinner sing-song voice.

"A carrot with a split pea for a bean," answers one of the shrimps.

*

I'm absolutely stuffed—and yet I go back for more. I go back for more because, although I'm not hungry, I'm nervous. And I'm nervous BECAUSE I'M ALIVE!

Les Lésions en Éspace

La mère de nos environs soniques-sociales
La plupart dur sel atomique ordonne
Ses élèves, qui grimpent soleil
Comme si la vecelle survivait cuit vive

La vecelle roulant ses seins bopées sur l'enfant
De sortilege, l'enfant qui remplace ses jambes
De pureé avec des jumping jambes de politesse

Abondant et bondant à travers des champs plastiques-fluids
Qui bagnent les lésions en éspace
Avec la profonde humidité d'une peine idiote

Lésions qui ont bousculaient les oeufs durs de succes
Qui remontent vers la plate planète
D'une poinçonneuse psychologique, comme when sa mère
Rit totalement à haute voix tout musicalement
Le nom de son futur enfant, au lieu de giving birth
                    to him at all

The Easter Island Situation

Stone giants keep watch over a landscape peopled
By hypertense distracted spooks

Spooks who monitor the peons working the land
And the workers who toil in office buildings

By means of an invisible calibrated rod
Hung from that point inside their bellies

Where the head pivots lightly from
The fulcrum of their days

The Golden Age of the Soviet Union

Learn to distinguish between language and thought, truth and logic, beauty and despair.

Take a hairpin and burst the magic bubble in the meat loaf.

Take twelve dozen hard boiled eggs and bring to bear upon them a vigorous chopping motion, and a gallon of mayonnaise. And don't forget the salt.

To get into the next attraction—an inflated bubble containing five talking dummies—one must obtain from the machine for 25 cents a brightly colored box with a message about drugs on the back.

Even more startling is the discovery that all the dummies—an American Indian, a black man, a housewife, a hippie and a Burmese woman—

From a loudspeaker above one hears appropriate folk tunes, including a German ditty about a Dr. Eisenbart who sings that he "gave ten pounds of opium to a flea circus and watched that whole scene."

Around the top of a vending machine, a moving ribbon of illuminated words conveys information about drugs. It employs all the devices of classical art, commercial art, pop art and graphic arts—plus neon lighting, vending machines and folk music. Plus folk tunes and vending machines.

The visitor is attracted to a 60-foot-high column whose four sides are illuminated in flashing red, green, blue and yellow lights spelling out the word DRUG.

It was just so completely stupid I couldn't believe it. It was a golfer's paradise.

Sensitivity Ode

Nothing's left today. A posteriori. Only what's behind survives
Since none of the new analogues require or support real substance.
The old magnet, to take your hand and stand your mute sensation,
Not even needing to agree, because you share community,
                    is gone . . .
Furthermore, you don't even begin to realize
How impossibly oversensitive you still are about all this:
When you look up, now, into Mother Nature's face
To drink and eat and pay for her magic
With your grace, she's looking right along with you—
And who can see that kind of face?

Which is how you conclude this season, with her
Sitting on your face, sensationally heavy but also elusive
And lost. As for everyone else, why if they're nice
They come close to you with money, just enough to get along.
                    Obviously not greedy,
You've simply mastered the necessary modesty and balance
Of enthusiastic curiosity protected by casual self-control—

    The struggle's always muted in most of this
    You sense simplicity in all there is to know

    The rest is deeper—it follows and precedes you
    It vibrates like a jelly as you come and go

The Glass Enclosure

Glassine envelopes trampoline the pigmeat into a final awakening.
It is the greater awakening. It is bleeding, bubbling and runny and
                                   it's funny that way.
The plastic knife acts extra-friendly today.
The matching plastic spoon and fork look on.
The paper plate pronounces a complete cellophane word.
The little girl treads water at the surface of a public moat
Its spidery fretwork of styrofoam roots supporting a bed
Of swirling metal apples whose hot white crust rides free.
And from the great unknown above her an ancient pie crust
Encloses a squirt of apple juice that hops and skips
Up the lovely burnished golden legs & down the silver-alloy arms
Of that greater fraction of young people
Required to strip themselves of their spirit and flee.
Their denouement comes at the moment of interment.

*

They cried like abandoned babies, who did not want to have to go
                                   through with this:
It is a black lump of coal in the throat
It is a miner's lamp of circumspection
It is the succulent baby checkerboard we pour milk on,
Milk as rich as eggs whose yolks of promise ride the air:
A stringy richness wrapping up the heart lies stricken there.
Its apoplectic textures weave a smack.
. . . While deep underground the railroadmen we love so, wearing their
distinctive hats like inverted maple syrup buckets and biting into huge
lunchbuckets, are gone from us forever.
The trains themselves don't anymore seem to work at all either,
Or if they do it's only up and down that they work, these trains—
Up and down from the eggs to the mines.

*

And the filling station too is filling up;
The glassine dogs play hurriedly with their envelopes,
Afraid the noise their shapes call forth
Will crack the dogs their noses bring, like a familiar glass person
Whose blithe, living spirit intersects its mechanical amble
And fills your smoky questioning hole with soda water:
The man who slew the dragon is selling used cars on the corner.

But that only happens later, after you've contemplated
The glass enclosure in your full maturity, and come to the following
Tentative set of conclusions:
1.—That the wigs turning discreetly in their shop window are
                                    turning for you,
Turning and turning on their trim white plastic heads.
2.—That the glass envelope briskly rubbed back and forth aborigine-style
Will set the palm of your hand on fire.
3.—That the clumsy message in the child's hot brain was freeze-dried
By the sets of ambidextrous parasols that rows of parents wield,
Who sweetly but firmly move forward to shield their children from
                        the rays that beat down and bounce up,
Discharging twinkling sunlight into the lamps of the afternoon . . .
The one random child whose freedom was made the exception to
                                    this rule
Set fire to the hand that fed him and is now but rarely seen,
An errant satellite consuming itself in the heavens above the glass.
You look up at dusk and see a tiny speck of smack
Relaying satellite-type information to his earth and fantasizing the rest.
4.—That in the best of all possible worlds every neighborhood would
have several restaurants like this one, each sunk in its own tradition, a
little island of simple ethnicity carefully preserving its methods and
standards amid its metropolitan reduction to eccentricity.

5.—That your two coaxial eyeballs search feverishly for a pair of breasts
to alight upon, a hand to hold.
6.—That a serenely academic pair of breasts now wears eyeglasses
To better verify the torrent of deeply-felt emotions
Their quivering nipples must sacrifice to a briskly changing scene:
First it is a mechanical millionaire, then a truckload of oppressed
                         migrant workers, then a busy city street.
Now it is a teetering office tower filling up with workers
From the street. They are white-collar workers who eye the giant
                         breast uncomfortably,
And their collars, though lately daringly and even arrogantly
Stained with fiery tabasco sauce, still retain
Their essential ancient stiffness and secret pain—
It is much too tight, the veins on the neck protrude, the forehead's
                         red and bulging, but very few complain.
The toasters heat up in the morning, the washer-dryers whir at night.
. . . And this a good dozen years after incoherent long-haired cartoon
characters invaded the confines of the Institute and ran screaming and
leering down its antiseptic white halls, disrupting the pools of typists at
their task by spraying them with chemicals that ran their stockings and
turned their brisk, prim statutory activities into a comic opera night-
mare!
No wonder these ruthless noisy little ruffians were reviled and shat
                         upon!
Yes, the collar is too tight but the majority cannot complain
Since if they did, their open necks would in short order
Burn closed forever in a sort of coppery-red tropical luncheon meat
Located bleeding quietly and compulsively in the mud beneath the
                         stairs:
At least, "The Face In The Carpet" swears such a grisly fate is theirs.

*

And believe it or not, this queer myth still persists in minds and
                    hearts today.
To me, it is a sub-picturesque or post-picturesque way of delaying
                    their departure
Until a combination Metaphysical Interior–and–Small Arms Factory
                    can be erected on the site
To house and occupy the horde of red-blooded workers inside the
                    great glass interior
That owes its existence to one architect's monumental homesickness:
He is wasting away his epic lung capacity on tiny numbered cubicles,
Lost like a broken toaster in the Valley of the Furniture Movers.
He contemplates with proud disdain the infinite functional anaconda
                    of garbage and noise that encircles him.
He disquiets the glass enclosure by abandoning his blueprint and
                    embracing messy self-disclosure instead.
Low rumbles are heard in the distance, seismic tremors, and for the
                    first time
Dust settles on the massive octagonal panes.
Two or three of the limitless glass molecules are cracked.

The Process: A Piece of Invective

> There is a life apart from politics: it is this life that the youth as virile poet lives in a kind of radiance and productive atmosphere. The pleasure that the poet has there is a pleasure of agreement with the radiant and productive world in which he lives.
>
> —Wallace Stevens, *The Life of the Poet*

THINK OF the personal situation of the poet in society today as an existence in some sort of vacant archetypal lock or position of unknowable dimensions. He or she is an ambiguous creature by definition, because he persists in doing something—in giving his life-energy to something—which is not defined as valuable. His activity is meaningless from the prevalent highly acquisitive, product-property-status point of view, unless he can sell himself like a circus lady in a zoo, journeying far from home in a woolen poncho with Indian feathers in his hair and so on.

A paradoxical result of his basic invisibility and social worthlessness is that a process is set in motion whereby the poet finds himself playing a heroic role in spite of himself: he becomes the homeless perennial wanderer, the one who won't fit in. If his tribal ancestors were shamans and singers whose contribution—the elaboration of their state of mind— played a valuable role in their respective cultures, he must reconcile himself today with existing on the borderline of playing any role at all. Anything magical the poet has to say is purely incidental to American life, the only ray of light being that the process at work on the poet still leaves him free to create if he accepts it. In this one respect it is more benign than the related process at work in society at large, whose members leave childhood behind to clamp onto their compulsive and routine adult identities. The poet in some cases barely escapes starvation, but on the other hand the cost of paper is cheap.

The last straw being that time magnifies and distorts this process, exaggerating rather than smoothing its impact. As the years go by matters get worse. He is "teaching in a university" now, we hear. Or driving a taxi "to make ends meet."

"This process" . . . I can't find the right words. Do I mean the person himself, or what is done to him by the squashing-machine of cultural reality and biological time?

All I know for certain is that—in society at large—this clamping down, this unremitting pressure that constricts free spirits into iron moulds of career, classification of self and acquisition of property, by the mere fact of its occurrence defines and justifies itself in the eyes of literally everyone. And it does so without cease. This overwhelming force grows in intensity as youth is left further and further behind and the "men and women" in us emerge, freshly baked and as it were freshly awakened. Unswervingly convinced their heavy metal identities have been with them all along. Not even aware, many of them, of the momentous *changes* in their personalities. Different people overnight. Suddenly youth is over.

And then what about the people who do realize to a more or less foggy extent what has come to pass? How long can they hold out? What chance do they stand compared with the pervasive nature of the forces arrayed against them? What are their feelings as they daily pass the magic barrier of awareness and see the zombie magnetism surrounding them that quietly awaits their surrender?

And finally, even the very small number of people who *do* escape after all, those whose lives remain fluid and whose sense of themselves is open and free to change: don't they become known as such and carefully and thoroughly classified as such, by others, forever? To take an example from the world of art, what did Marcel Duchamp do when he realized his role-image (which amused him no end) had become famous in the meantime and could even (wonder of wonders) keep him economically self-sufficient the rest of his life so long as he didn't rock the boat? So long as he remained Marcel Duchamp. Did he make the conscious decision at some point to go on being "Marcel Duchamp"? Or did he see that he was non-existent to the extent that he conformed to the image others had of him, even if that image included charming non sequiturs, hysterical amusements, unexpected gestures and the like?

At what point did M.D. cease being M.D. while still being M.D.? Was he the same as before?

His image exists forever, then—it is posthumous—while Marcel himself sits before us (say all this takes place on a warm, rainy morning in June, 1918) puffing on his pipe and smiling to himself as he dusts off a rook.

Mentioning only Duchamp in this connection does not, of course, exclude anyone else from the ravages of the process, to a greater or lesser degree, all the way from Gerald Ford to Lou Reed and including in fact the rest of us as well.

We seem to be sliding into these masks, as if rolling or tumbling in slow motion into immobility—a "delay in glass" as Duchamp put it. Sliding or tumbling into a frozen turquoise statue of options, identity, modes of behavior and idiosyncrasies that altogether go to make up John or Jane Doe.

. . . Observed, physiologically-speaking, in the gradual stiffening with age of the collagen, the mortar of the cells . . .

* * *

Among the preponderance of the total population afflicted with what still can accurately be termed petty bourgeois desires, this process manifests itself in (among other things) an obsessive craving for the acquisition of personal property, as if its sheer weight alone will make them real. Literal property (house, cars, real estate, lawn mowers, family, all seeming to shout aloud: "See, it's me! I exist!") as well as the accumulation of money, social status and personal power. That's what many people on this highly evolved planet spend their lives doing, assuming they're not among the hopelessly poverty-stricken or mentally-stricken and consequently unable to get the ball rolling.

But ultimately there's no standing aside from this process. It's tied up in some powerful way with the very fact of time passing. It seems to spare no one, turning sweet young family men into secret ravening sensualists, all in the flick of a hat, and bringing bitterness and premature death to the middle-in-years. It is a sudden, stark tearing-away motion, like an elaborate costume of torture suddenly, dramatically and provocatively torn away from the flesh; which is also precisely the motion, though in this case clogged with passion, whose tactile thrill gives goosebumps to all the secret swingers among us with sexy decayed breath, a sizable and growing element of our "American" population. Changing their masks once a week for the thrill, a thrill so divine they want to do it again and again. Or not wearing the darn thing at all for a while, which this time around usually takes the form of in L.A. with dark glasses, smiling too often to themselves as they stumble up Malibu Beach, drink in hand, toward a grand apotheosis of rare sirloin and soft, plump, purple whiskers in the sunset . . . Another quart of vodka, please . . .

But this tipsy funnel or channel or walkway through reality is just one aspect of the entire elusive problem confronting us as a society. Idle questions about "what is art" or "what is poetry" pale before its magnitude, although one related question does remain, even growing in importance as the elements of the major difficulty fall into place. Namely, the question of bad poetry remains—i.e., what is bad poetry, and what is there to do about it, and especially what is there to do about it when it occurs in conjunction with one of those touchy "men and women"? But although this may be a serious philosophical problem,

concerning as it does the limitation of knowledge of others and of one-
self, and also the necessity of getting along with others as you would
have them get along with you—nevertheless, it calls forth too many
shimmering wraiths to be dealt with by the light of day.

Rather spare the poets for once, I hear a voice inside me saying, and
inquire instead about the vast horde of sleepers encased in their masks
in this world, and the venial malevolence of some of them, and why—
century after century—the narrow, the corrupt or the cruel continue to
rule it. Who or what gave them this right? Is it simply a matter of cer-
tain character types recurring again and again throughout history? And
finally should I, as a poet, stand still for them? How should I respond to
them when their bureaucratic contingent says to me, for example:
"You are a poet. You will proceed to Room 181-A to learn the pre-
scribed manner for teaching poetry to children." (Or as someone said
to me seriously not long ago: "You're a poet. How come you wrote a
novel?")

In other words, "He is a poet: he sticks it in the mailbox." He is
not simply alive on this earth, to sit and think, or go for a walk (for a
week). He cannot simply fly and walk. He'll become a "beachcomber"
if he does that. A recluse. Or worse. The lonely destiny of the drifter.
To go from one suit of clothes to another. For he too, in the end, will be
conked out by the process. "I pressed rich cheeses for the ungrateful
town," as Virgil said. But that's okay: at least he won't go out in per-
manent press.

Printed in Lunenburg, Vermont, in November 1975
by The Stinehour Press. Designed by Freeman Keith.
This edition is limited to 1500 copies,
of which 26 are lettered and signed.